Faith's Vision

I0182755

See Yourself & See the World the Way God Sees Us!

Rudi Louw

Copyright © 2014 by Rudi Louw Publishing

All rights reserved solely by the author. No part of this book may be reproduced in any form *without the permission of the author.*

Most Scripture quotations are taken from the *Revised Standard Version*, Holy Bible, Thomas Nelson Publishers. Copyright © 1983 by Thomas Nelson, Inc.

Some Scripture quotations were taken from the *New King James Version*, Holy Bible, Thomas Nelson Publishers. Copyright © 1983 by Thomas Nelson, Inc.

All Scripture quotations not taken from the RSV, or NKJV are a literal translation of the Scriptures.

The Holy Scriptures are just that, HOLY.

Statements enclosed in brackets were inserted into Scripture quotations to add emphasis or clarify the meaning of what is being said in those scriptures. The integrity of God's Word to man was not compromised in any way. Due care and diligence was cautiously exercised to keep the Word of Truth intact.

For example: The apostle Paul said in his second letter to Timothy in chapter three verse sixteen that:

"All Scripture is given by inspiration of God (literally God breathed)*, and is profitable for doctrine, for reproof, for correction, for instruction **in righteousness**,"* NKJV

Contents

The Marvel of the Holy Bible

1. Uninterrupted Theme and Inspired Thought

It took *1,500 years* to compile the Holy Bible, involving *more than 40 different authors*. <u>Yet</u> the theme and inspired thought of Scripture continues *uninterrupted* from author to author, from beginning till end.

2. Absence of Mythical Stories

Compare philosophies and theories about creation in the Middle East, Europe, Asia, Africa, and Latin America and you'll find mythical scenarios: gods feuding and cutting up other gods to form the heavens and the earth, etc.

In ancient Greek mythology, the Greeks see Atlas carrying the earth on his shoulders. In India, Hindus believe eight elephants carry the earth on their backs.

But in contrast, Job, the oldest book in the Holy Bible, declares that, *"God suspends the earth on nothing."(Job 26:7)*

This was said millennia before Isaac Newton discovered the invisible laws of gravity that delicately balance every planet and sun in its individual circuit.

Contrary to every other ancient attempt to give a creation account, *the Holy Bible pictures the creation of the earth in a very scientific manner.*

For example, in Genesis Chapter One, the continents are lifted from the seas, then vegetation is formed and later animal life, all reproducing *'according to its own kind'*, **thus recognizing the fixed genetic laws.** In addition, we have the bringing forth of man and woman, *all done by God in a dignified and proper manner, without mythological adornments.*

The balance or remainder of the Holy Bible follows suite.

The narratives are **true historical documents**, *faithfully reflecting society and culture* **as history and archaeology would discover them thousands of years later. Not only is the Holy Bible historically accurate, it is also reliable when it deals with scientifically proven subjects.** It was never intended to be a textbook on history, science, mathematics, or medicine. *However, when its writers touch on these subjects,* **they often state facts that scientific advancement would not reveal, or even consider, until thousands of years later.**

While many have doubted the accuracy of the Holy Bible, time and continued research have consistently demonstrated that the Word of God is better informed than its critics.

3. Intactness

Of all the ancient works of substantial size, *the Holy Bible survives intact, against all odds and expectations.*

Compared with other ancient writings, the Holy Bible has more manuscripts as evidence to support it than any ten pieces of classical literature combined!

The plays of William Shakespeare, for instance, were written about four hundred years ago, after the invention of the printing press. Many of his original writings and words have been lost in numerous sections, *yet the Holy Bible's uncanny preservation has weathered thousands of years of wars, contradictions, persecutions, fires and invasions.*

Through the centuries Jewish scribes have preserved the Holy Bible's Old Covenant text, ***such as no other manuscripts have ever been preserved. They kept tabs on every letter, syllable, word and paragraph.*** *They continued from generation to generation to appoint and train special groups of men within their culture* ***whose sole duty it was to***

preserve and transmit these documents <u>with perfect accuracy and fidelity</u>.

Who ever bothered to count the letters, syllables, or words of Plato, Aristotle, or Seneca for that matter?

When it comes to the New Testament, the actual number of preserved manuscripts is so great that it becomes overwhelming. ***There are more than 5,680 Greek manuscripts, more than 10,000 Latin Vulgate manuscripts and at least 9,300 other versions. Further still, there exists an additional 25,000 manuscript copies of portions of the New Testament.*** **No other document of antiquity even begins to approach such numbers.**

The closest in comparison is Homer's <u>Iliad</u>, with only 643 manuscripts. The first complete work of Homer only dates back to the 13th century.

4. Unmatched Accuracy in Predictive Foretelling

The Holy Bible is unmatched in accuracy in predictive foretelling. No other ancient work succeeds in this or even begins to attempt this.

Other books such as the Koran, the Book of Mormon, and parts of the Veda claim divine inspiration; ***but none of these books contain predictive foretelling.***

This one undeniable fact we know for certain: *While microscopic scrutiny would show up the imperfections, blemishes, and defects of any work of Man, <u>it magnifies the beauties and perfection of God</u>. Just as every flower displays in accurate detail the reflection and perfection of beauty, <u>so does the Word of Truth when it is scrutinized</u>.*

Historian Philip Schaff wrote:

*"Without money and weapons, Jesus the Christ conquered more millions than Alexander, Caesar, Mohammad, and Napoleon. Without science and learning, He (Jesus the Christ) shed more light on things human and divine than all philosophers and scholars combined. Without the eloquence of schools, He (Jesus the Christ) spoke such words of life as was never spoken before or since and produced effects which lie beyond the reach of orator or poet. Without writing a single line, He (Jesus the Christ) set more pens in motion and furnished themes for more sermons, orations, discussions, learned volumes, works of art, and songs of praise **than the whole army of great men of ancient and modern times combined.**"* (*The Person of Christ*, p33. 1913)

Today, there are literally billions of Bibles in more than 2,000 languages.

Isn't it about time you find out what it really has to say?

Hey listen, the Holy Bible is all about Jesus, the Messiah, the Christ…

…and everything about Jesus Christ is really about YOU!!

Study Tips:

Read 2 Corinthians 5:14, 16, 18, 19, and 21.

In the light of these Scriptures, it should be obvious that, if you want to study the Holy Bible, *you should study it in the light of Mankind's redemption!*

Feed daily on **redemption realities** found in the book of Acts, in Romans Chapters One through Eight, and in Ephesians, Colossians, and Galatians, also in 1 Peter Chapter One, 2 Peter Chapter One, James Chapter One, as well as in 1 and 2 Corinthians.

Acknowledgments

I want to acknowledge and thank one of my mentors in the faith, Francois du Toit, for blessing and impacting me with revelation knowledge.

I borrowed the portion on *"The Marvel of the Holy Bible"* from his website: http://www.MirrorWord.net, as students so often feel they have a right to do with things that come from teachers they respect. Just as Galatians 6:6 says, *"Let him who is taught the Word **share in all good things** with him who teaches."*

To all our dear friends and family, for all the love and support, and to all those who helped me with this project:

THANK YOU!

Also, especially to my wife, Carmen;

For keeping me genuine by being my companion in life and partner in ministry,

I love and appreciate you so very much!

Foreword

Thank you for taking the time to read this book.

Let me start off by saying that *I am totally addicted to my Daddy's love for me.*

I am in love with Jesus Christ, *and that is enough for me!*

The love of God is so much more than a doctrine, a philosophy, or a theory. It is so much more and goes so much deeper than knowledge; it way surpasses knowledge.

We are talking heart language here.

I write *to impact people's hearts,* to make them see the mysteries that have been hidden in Father God's heart concerning Christ Jesus, and actually *concerning THEM,* so as to arrest their conscience with it, *that I may introduce them to their original design and to their true selves,* **and present them to themselves perfect in Christ Jesus** *and set them apart unto Him **in love**,* as a chaste virgin.

We are involved with the biggest romance of the ages!

Therefore this book cannot be read as you would a novel: *casually.* It is not a cleverly devised little myth or fable. **It contains**

revelation into some things you may or may not have considered before.

It is the TRUTH of God, ultimate TRUTH, and therefore has direct bearing upon YOUR life. **The Word and the Spirit are my witness** *to the reality of these things!*

Be like the people of Berea whom the apostle Paul ministered to in Acts 17:11. Open yourself up to study the revelation contained in this book **to discover for yourself the reality of these things**.

Be forewarned! Do not become guilty of the sins of the Pharisees, **or you too will miss out on the depth of fulfillment God Himself, who is LOVE, wants to give** <u>**YOU**</u>.

Jesus said of the Pharisees and Sadducees that they strain out every little gnat BUT swallow whole camels. What He meant by that is that *some people seem to have it all together when it comes to doctrine and they love to argue.*

It makes them feel important, but it is nothing other than EMPTY religious and intellectual pride.

They know the Scriptures in and out, and YET they are still so IGNORANT about **REAL TRUTH that is only found in LOVE.**

They are still so ignorant and indifferent **towards the things that REALLY MATTER.**

14

They are always arguing over the use of *every little jot and tittle* and over the meaning and interpretation of *every word of Scripture.*

The exact thing they accuse everyone else of doing though, the precise thing they judge everyone else for, *they are actually doing themselves.* That is **they often downright misinterpret and twist what is being said, *making a big deal of insignificant things while obscuring or weakening God's real truth: the truth of His LOVE*.**

*They are always majoring on minors **<u>because they do not understand the heart of God</u>** and therefore they constantly miss the whole point of the message.*

Paul himself said it so beautifully,

*"...the letter kills but **the Spirit BRINGS LIFE**;"*

*"...<u>knowledge puffs up</u>, but **LOVE EDIFIES**."*

I say again:

Allow yourself to get caught up in the revelation I am about to share.

Open yourself up to study the insight contained in this book, *not only with a desire to gain knowledge, but also with anticipation **to hear from Father God yourself, to encounter Him through His Word, and to embrace truth, in order to know and believe the LOVE God has for <u>you</u>***, *so that you may get so caught up* in it, *that you too may receive from Him LOVES' impartation of LIFE.*

This revelation contains within it the voice and call of LOVE Himself to every human being on the face of this earth. *If you take heed to it, and yield yourself fully to it, **it is custom designed and guaranteed to forever alter and enrich your life!***

"Of His own will (passionate desire)
He brought us forth (from)
(and) **by the word of truth**
that we should **be** (exist as)
a kind of first fruits
of His creatures!"

"But be doers (believers) of the word
and not mere hearers
only deceiving yourselves;
For if anyone is (only) a hearer
of the word, and not a doer (a believer)

(our doing is only the fruit of our understanding & believing)

...he is like a man who observes the face of his birth (or **origin** – thus his **true** face) **as in a mirror but** (he things it's too good to be true, so he rejects it, and) he **goes away** (he goes back to his old way of seeing himself) **and at once forgets** (he puts out of his mind on purpose) **what kind of man he is** (as revealed in the Word of Truth, or Mirror Message)"

– James 1:18-24

Prayer

Father thank you for Your eternal Word!

We thank you that what You have given us in Your Word is greater and larger than what any season could contain!

Father it's larger than the old year past, and it's greater and larger than this New Year coming!

So we thank you and we bless You **for the fact that we may interpret our lives,** *no longer in terms of seasons that come and go; no longer in terms that calendars can calculate!*

Father we thank you that our life has become *the life of God in Christ;* that life that You have given us through Your eternal Word made flesh in Jesus Christ!

And Father we thank you that our celebration, Father, is the celebration of that incarnate Word; *the incarnation of Your Logos!*

Father we thank you that our lives have become that Word; *that Logos extended in this life!*

Father, so as we get into the topic of this book together, and into the Scriptures, *we thank you for the unction of the Holy Spirit upon the Word of God!*

Father we thank you *for inspired expression!*

Father as I sit here and I write, *I am conscious of the Holy Spirit illuminating my understanding to write the oracles, the utterances; the very expression of God Himself!*

Father, the precious folks that picked up this book to read, *did not pick it up to simply read a man-made essay, but Father both they and I have a hunger in our hearts to once again tap into, and dive into, the eternal limitless resources of the eternal limitless God; the very God who expressed Himself, not merely in the Scriptures, but in the Word made flesh!*

We thank you that we may take counsel from You right now, oh God!

Thank you that You have become our Great Counselor!

Thank you that You have made Your wisdom known, and that You in Christ have become wisdom unto us!

Thank you for that wisdom Father God; *Your wisdom!*

Thank you that You have given us Your Word, and Your mind and Your heart.

Thank you that You have disclosed it in the Scriptures for us to discover!

And so Father, I pray that as people read this book, and Your Scriptures expounded on in here, *they will be fully conscious of the fact* that they are not dealing with, and having to make do with, the mere letters of Man's writings and philosophies,

I pray Father that they would recognize that they are dealing with the God who desires to communicate and reveal His heart to all mankind!

So Father, I pray that they too will begin to treasure Your word *as their greatest wealth, simply because, Father, of the fact that we have no treasure in this world that can equal what You have given us in Christ Jesus; the Word made flesh!*

Thank you for the treasure that is ours in the word made flesh!

Thank you that the Scriptures are Your roadmap to it, and so Your word has also been made flesh in us, for we have heard, and we have seen, and gazed upon in amazement, and we have also experienced tangibly for ourselves that Word of life!

And Father, those of us who have seen these things so clearly, are overwhelmed with thanksgiving and appreciation and adoration of

You, *for that Word of Life truly has become our own testimony!*

And so, Father, this book then is my testimony of these things, and I worship You Father for it, and I worship You with it!

Amen!

Chapter 1

Consider God's Anticipation for Your Life!

Well, let me start off by saying that in the beginning of a new year *the best thing you can do is to consider the year in the light of God's anticipation for your life!* And so I want to talk to you in this book about Faith's vision!

I praise God that faith can find expression in vision! Because faith without vision would just implode and self-destruct. But I thank God that when faith catches vision it is left with no choice, *it will simply have to EXPLODE!*

So watch out all you religious devils! Ha... ha... ha...

Sure it will explode! *It will have no choice!* That is if we are talking about a kind of faith that is similar to that which God exercises, *and especially when we start talking about, and thinking in terms of, the very faith of God Himself!*

That faith of God, whether it is found in God or in us, generates God's energy and His limitless creative ability!

It is therefore that very explosive element, *that very faith of God,* that I desire us to talk about and consider in this book together!

I want us to measure together, not merely our vision for ourselves and for our ministry, but I want us to measure together **God's vision** for our lives and for our ministry right here in 2014 and then in 2015 and beyond!

I thank God that we no longer need to allow ourselves *to be intimidated by anything that the future holds for natural man **because we are not mere men!***

Hallelujah!

We are so much more!

I thank God that we have the privilege to discover the vision of ourselves that God's Word inspires!

In Proverbs 29:18 we read that,

"…a people without vision parishes;"

"…they are a people who cast off their focus, self-control and restraint or inhibitions, and abandon themselves to a mere insignificant life in the flesh!"

That's exactly what happens when you are dealing with inferior faith; *with man-made faith **that has no real God inspired vision.***

Let me tell you straight: **It will self-destruct and implode on you like man-made religious ideas, philosophies, and doctrines always do!**

But I do thank God that His Word of truth, the gospel of our salvation, *inspires the kind of vision* **that will satisfy both His heart and the heart of the believer!**

Faith's vision *is a focus on eternal realities!*

You see if the enemy can keep occupying your mind *with temporal things* **then he can rob you of the quality year that God has in mind for you!**

And let me tell you; *that year is not measured the same way you look at a year on a natural calendar!* No, that year's measure is determined *by what you and I can see and can say now!* It's determined by what we can *continue to see and keep saying.*

Our years' measure then, our experience in it *is defined* **by what we can maintain in our vision and sustain in our confession; our conversation!**

You see we daily take a portion at a time; *we take it, we take our day, and we take what we can see; that reality in the spirit,* **and we lay a hold of it in the now,** *and we say, 'God this is Your day, this is Your time, I give it to You. I am Yours and You are mine and there is no separation between us; use me in the NOW!'*

25

You know, the privilege of the believer is that **we partake of eternal life!** And you see, eternity is larger than time. Time exists within eternity *and eternity governs it!*

I want you to know that eternal life is not just a concept, *it is a revelation of a life quality that is greater and bigger than time!*

And so if we approach this year we live in, and this coming year also, in the faith that God desires to quicken within us, *His faith, then we will see in this year and in the years to come,* not obstacles and restrictions, *but opportunities and possibilities, larger than what we could ever dream of in the natural!*

I want you as individual believers, and us together as a body of believers, as the body of Christ, to ask ourselves the question today: What is God able to accomplish through our lives this year *in the light of His investment in us?*

I mean, what can He accomplish in the light of His investment on my behalf, _and really, His investment within me_?

Please make that the question of your heart!

Make this your prayer: *'God, what are You able to communicate through my life in this year, _in the light of Your investment in me_?'* *And then also **allow the Holy Spirit to help you answer that question!***

26

I had a wonderful conversation on my cellphone, just this morning, with a very excited young man. You know, many of his friends had written him off and told me how he was the biggest rebel around. But listen, he got a hold of the revelation of grace and its redemption realities, and then God got a hold of him and did something marvelous within him through that truth, through His love, *and it transformed him.* And he started reading our books available online, and he told me this morning how he honed in on one of our messages on: *"Seeing Jesus."* I don't even remember in which book I focused on that message, probably all of them, ha... ha... ha... but he said to me, *'As I read that book, the glory of God appeared to me in my room.'*

Ha... ha... ha... isn't that something!?

Now according to him he had such an encounter there with God in the privacy of his bedroom. So much so that the next day that same friend, who had previously written him off and told him that he was the biggest rebel and greatest loser around, came to him and asked him, *'Man, what happened to you? Something is different about you. You are a totally different person now. Come on; tell us what happened to you!'*

Apparently his face was literally radiant with love and joy; with the very testimony of God concerning him in Christ Jesus!

He told me that since that day he has been preaching everywhere, every day. He said it has been rather embarrassing to watch what happens every time, because there has been some opposition, and if I remember our conversation correctly, one of the teachers at the college he attends, and even his boss at work, warned the other students and the other co-workers, *'Now, don't listen to this guy too much because we are Christians too, and this guy, he is too much of a heretic and a fanatic for Jesus.'* *'But,'* he says, *'It didn't work.'*

Ha... ha... ha...

They were not able to affect anything or change anyone's mind about him, because the more they tried to stop the rest from listening to him, the more those people just wanted to hear more of what he had to say, *because there was something so beautiful and attractive in it that they couldn't help but be drawn by it;* **by the love contained in the simple gospel message** he brought.

He told me how he was, just a few days prior to our conversation, invited by one of the dorm room leaders of the college to come and address a gathering of students at the dorm room. When he got there, there were more than 500 students from all kinds of religious and non-religious backgrounds gathered to hear him. He said they had such an anointed time together full of inspiration that many approached him after his talk and felt compelled just to say to him, *'You know, we have never heard the gospel in this way before and it's blowing our minds! We are just captivated by the love of God, man! Tell us where we can get a hold of more resources and material with this emphasis on the gospel!'*

So as a result, apparently all kinds of doors are now opening up for him to come and share everywhere, and even some churches have started asking him to come and share with their youth, and some even in their main Sunday morning services.

Wow! Isn't it amazing?!

And you know; I so enjoyed him and what he was sharing with me on that cellphone, about how that revelation of God's investment in his life, as well as in every one of our lives, has so transformed him. It was such a joy, and I couldn't help but get overwhelmed with him in fellowship, as we appreciated together, the grace of God, and that investment in our lives through that marvelous work of redemption!

And what I was saying earlier is that, you know, as long as the enemy **can restrict you to what people say about you, even to what you think about yourself in the natural, or to what your diplomas and certificates, or the lack thereof, could say about you,** *then you will keep living an absolutely frustrated life!*

But listen, God desires for us *to discover the measureless dimensions of our identity*

29

in Christ Jesus. He desires for us to interpret our life in the light of that. He also desires for us to interpret 2014 and 2015 and beyond in the light of that, so that we can be elevated to a heavenly perspective, and be able to say, *'God Your dream for my life is indeed the fuel of my faith!'*

'Father, Your dream for my life is greater and more exciting, it is more than even my most positive anticipation for 2015 and beyond!'

'And Father I refuse to limit myself to any other opinion, and restrict myself by any other opinion!'

Hallelujah!

Praise God for such a heavenly perspective, *for His perspective of us* and of our lives!

Chapter 2

The Gospel Reveals Your Mirror Image Clearly!

James 1:22,

"But be doers (believers) *of the word and not* (merely) *hearers* (of it), *only deceiving yourselves…"*

Did you know that your encounter of the Word can be limited to a mere sermon that you hear? It can even be a wonderful, positive message! But listen, God has more in mind for you than just another message, or even just another challenge to your faith. God's challenge that He brings to us in His Word is to generate within us a new kind of action, and that action is based upon the next verse.

He says,

"For if anyone is (merely) *a hearer of the word, and not* (also) *a doer* (a believer, actively believing; truly believing)…"*

I want us to really consider this verse because so often we have read this verse in the light of the Old Covenant, with a works-mindset, and we got all caught up in that legalistic Law mentality again of, *'I've got to become a DOER of the word, or else!'* and then we feel all guilty and condemned again. Listen, if you do that you might as well just go read the Law and go back to the time of the Law, *and just begin to focus again on, 'Do this!' and 'Don't do that!' ...And somehow those dos and don'ts are now supposed to please God ...but there is no faith in that!*

But hey, that is not what these New Testament Scriptures say! This scripture in James speaks here *of the secret, the mystery of* **the action of revelation knowledge within you.** *It speaks of* **what that revelation knowledge into the faith of God releases in you to do.** It speaks of revelation into the word; into the incarnation, into the word made flesh; into the very faith of God revealed! **That revelation into redemption,** *releases an action within you! It's an action taken by the Word; by the very faith of God at work within you, which releases you both to will and to do of what His good pleasure ...of what His faith, reveals!*

That action begins with your accurate hearing and comprehending!

James 1:23,

"For if anyone is a (mere) *hearer of the word and not a doer* (a believer)

...he is like a man who observes the face of his birth (of his **origin** – thus his **true** face; the face of his **true identity**) *as in a mirror..."*
32

In other words, he is like a man who hears the word of truth, and in the hearing of the gospel, in the hearing of the word of redemption, in the hearing of the word of Christ, *he observes the face of his birth, the face of his **origin** (**the face of his genesis in God,** says the Greek; the face of his **authentic original identity;** his **true identity**).

In the word of truth, in the word of Christ, in the gospel being observed, he sees, not just the face of Man's original design, the face of Man's original birth there in the garden, *but he observes the face of his own birth there in Christ in his work of redemption. He observes and sees the face of his own restoration back to his original design, back to his origin, back to that image and likeness of God in which he has been made, **that image and likeness that is within him already.*** He sees and observes his own restoration and reconciliation back to God, his true Father, there in the gospel, in the word of truth, in the word of Christ! He sees and observes his own restoration to his Daddy who loves him, and to eternal reality; to his true identity, there in the work of redemption; there in the work of Christ!

Verse 23 goes on to say,

"...and he observes himself (his true identity) ***as in a mirror,** but he observes* (casually or in a dismissive way, thinking that it's just too good to be true) *and he goes away* (back to his old way of seeing himself) ***and at once forgets***

33

(dismisses and puts out of his mind) *what he saw there in that mirror!"*

"...he forgets **(he dismisses and deliberately ignores)** *what he saw;"*

Or,

"...he **(simply over time)** *forgets* **(again)** *that image he saw of himself* **(his true identity)** *in the mirror!"*

"...he forgets <u>his true image</u> *he saw there ...his actual* **(authentic)** *image!"*

"...he forgets what he **(his true image)** *was actually truly like!"*

The enemy knows that the only way he can stop the purpose of God in the individual's life *is to get them sidetracked in their mind!*

The moment the word of truth, the word of Christ, the gospel, initiates God's vision of you in your life (God's sight), *there is a quickening; an activation by the Spirit of Truth, by the Spirit of God. There is a quickening; an activation of what has been dormant in you – a metamorphosis. It's a birth, a springing forth of new life within you!*

Hallelujah!

A whole new life is birthed within your comprehension and therefore also within your spirit! There is an awakening that takes place! I mean, you experience that truth coming alive in you, in your thinking, in your understanding, and then also therefore in your spirit; in your whole being. **You experience that new life, that life impartation coming from truth,** *awakening the true authentic original you* **within your inner being and so you see now a whole new life before you!**

You see, when I hear the word of truth, the word of Christ, the gospel of my salvation, *I* **see the face of my birth! I see my rebirth there in Him**, *in Christ, in that work of redemption,* **in His resurrection!**

Verse 18 of that same chapter speaks of how we are **brought forth** by the word of truth.

He says, *"Of His own will* (or by His own desire. In other words: In making His own will known, or, by making known to us what He knows; *by making known to us what He accomplished in Christ,* or, by making known to us what He accomplished by His own will, in Christ ...by making that desire and accomplishment known; by that will fulfilled and made know) **He brought us forth by that word of truth** (by the word of Christ; by the truth of the gospel) **that we should be a kind of first fruits of His creatures!"**

You see, if the enemy can now somehow interfere **with the <u>impact</u> of that word** upon my spirit, **with the _impact_ of the truth of that word** _upon my heart and upon my understanding,_ and get my mind occupied again with distractions and with some other subtle lies and deception, with earthly things, **_then I forget what manner of man I am!_**

I want to challenge you as you read this and I want to challenge us as a whole, as believers, as the body of Christ at large: **We cannot afford to forget what manner of man we are!**

We cannot afford to face the future **outside of this revelation; outside of what God revealed in redemption!** We cannot afford to face the future of the world **outside of this _ruling reality!_**

We cannot afford to face **our own future** _outside of this **ruling reality** of **who we are** in Christ Jesus; **the reality** of **who we really are, as revealed, in the face of Christ, and in the face of His mighty work of redemption; in the face of His mighty achievement in that work!**_

Perhaps one of the greatest verses of Scripture is found there in 2 Corinthians 3:18, where Paul talks about beholding Christ **_as in a mirror._**

He says, _"**Beholding** Him ...**as in a mirror,**_

...we are being changed (we are instantly transformed) _into His likeness..."_

Hey, don't get fooled now by the *"**are being changed**"* bit!

He meant that the change happens **instantly** as you realize that what you are beholding, *you are actually beholding within yourself, **as if looking into a mirror!***

Listen, that change only has to take *as long as it takes for revelation to **dawn** upon your understanding, to **penetrate your spirit**, to **penetrate your heart!*** That transformation and that change only takes as long as it takes for you **to believe** the truth, to **actually** believe it and **fully embrace it!** It doesn't have to be some long dragged out process. *Because you see, the transformation **happens in your thinking, in your heart.*** And then once your thinking, once your mindset is transformed, *once your thought process, your whole mentality about God and about yourself and about others and about life, has been changed and renewed through a revelation into the truth,* **your body and your conduct will automatically follow!** You see your life will then automatically, easily, line up **with what you really believe and think and embrace in your heart, in your spirit,** *in your inner being, in your thought-life!*

2 Corinthians 3:18,

***"Beholding Him as in a mirror, we are being changed** (instantly transformed) into His very likeness!"*

37

Listen, religion will keep you for years and years *sentimentally beholding Jesus, and thereby putting you in a position of beholding Him,* **as in a show window; instead of a <u>mirror</u>!**

Under religion we considered Christ, o yes we did, but we considered Him after the flesh; we considered His birth, and we considered His life, and we considered His death. So, we considered Him. We even considered His Lordship; the high and exalted One, above all else, and we even considered Him, as the WORD. So, yes, we even considered all the prophetic words; *we considered* **the WORD, <u>but not as in a mirror</u>**!

The WORD, the CHRIST; **that WORD** was something wonderful. It was something beautiful ...*but **just** beyond our reach!*

But no, **GOD says** that *as I consider Him, as you and I consider the WORD, as you consider Jesus,* **not only high up on some pedestal** *(He is that, amen),* **but also considering Jesus <u>in the mirror</u> of the word, there's a transforming power, an instantly transforming power released into our lives; into my life and your life!** *There's a power that transforms my mind, my thinking and my inner being <u>into His very likeness</u> as I am beholding Him <u>in the mirror</u> of the word!*

It transforms my inner being <u>into His image; His likeness</u>!

You know, even in our praise we have often wonderfully exalted Him! *But in our testimony we have belittled Him!* **We have failed to see ourselves in Him, and we have failed to see Him in us! We have failed to see Him <u>as in a mirror</u>!**

That means that *when I now look at Christ, **I am no longer able to look at Him independent of myself, as separate from me!***

I mean, *I am no longer able to consider the One who died 2,014 years ago* **without considering at the same time <u>the fact</u> *that I have been crucified together with Him, and was raised to newness of life, together with Him!***

Do you now see the difference between *the mirror* and the show window?

Hallelujah!

When I consider the fact that I have been associated in Christ and united with Him, in His death, *the power of the word, the power of that truth* **energizes my faith, *and I remember what manner of man I really am ...according to the face of my birth ...there in Him!***

Chapter 3

Stop Thinking Like Mere Men!

Let's quickly look at 1 Corinthians Chapter Three. It is difficult to interpret Chapter Three correctly without first comprehending Chapter Two, *so let me just refer to 1 Corinthians 2:6 quickly.*

Paul says,

"Yet among the mature we do impart wisdom, *although, it is not a wisdom* (it is not a ruling philosophy) *of this age, and it is not the wisdom of the rulers of this age, who are doomed to pass away;"*

*"…***but we impart a secret and hidden wisdom of God, which God decreed before the ages <u>for our glorification</u>.***"*

Paul speaks here of **a revelation** *that is communicated through the gospel.*

But now in Chapter 3 and Verse 1 he says,

"But I brethren could not address you as spiritual men; **but as men of the flesh,** *as babes in Christ!"*

Paul does not deny the fact that they had already been enlightened to some degree through the word that they had heard, and that they had already accepted the fact that Jesus is Lord, and obviously they have yielded to God to some degree and become Christians ...*but now Paul says to them that* **while we allow the mentality of ordinary things; of our natural identity, <u>to dominate us</u>,** *we fail to grasp the full implication of God's purpose with us in Christ; in His work of redemption, and in His plan for the restoration of all things to Himself,* **here** *at the end of the ages;* **in the here and now!**

So here in this Scripture Paul expresses a frustration with these people that he has in his ministry to them. He speaks about those who are mature as opposed to those who would prefer to remain in the flesh. He says that they remain in the flesh, not because time doesn't allow them to enter into what God has in mind for them, *nor because they haven't studied hard enough, or are simply not old enough, or even because there hasn't been enough time, or that time has anything to do with it.* **No, they remain in the flesh and do not enter into what God has for them** *because of foolishness in their own hearts!* **They restrict themselves** to natural mindedness, to natural minded things, to mere natural thinking and to natural things! They restrict themselves *to things,* Paul says, *that pertain to babes! They are like infants when it comes to spiritual things.*

He says, **They have no comprehension, no real interaction with God and spiritual things, and no consistency either, there, in that natural oriented mind-set!**

So Paul says to them that his desire is *to impart a wisdom, **a revelation,** into their minds and into their hearts and into their spirits!* He *wants to impart a* <u>revelation</u> **that will cause not only them, *but us,* to experience the full stature of Christ within us!**

And now he says here in 1 Corinthians 3:1,

"But I, could not address you as spiritual men, but as men of the flesh, as babes in Christ"

Verse 2,

"I fed you with milk and not with solid food, for you were not ready for it, and even yet you are not ready."

Why?

Verse 3,

"...for you are still of the flesh!"

Why?

"...for while there is jealousy and strife among you, are you not of the flesh,"

*"...and behaving **like ordinary Men**?"*

I want you to know that Paul refers here to Christians. They had become Christians after they heard the gospel, after they were enlightened to some degree through the word that was preached to them, and they had embraced the fact that Jesus is Lord, and had, therefore, yielded to God in their lives and had started living to some degree for Him who died for them! So Paul is referring here to believers, supposedly *"born again"*, sold-out Christians, **who were still behaving like ordinary Men;** *like ignorant unbelievers!*

He was actually saying, '**You are not ordinary Men!** *But in your actions your testimony is still restricted to the experience of an ordinary Man. In your behavior, in your thinking and in your conduct,* **you are still restricting your testimony to that of an ordinary Man!**'

He says in Verse 4,

"For when one says, 'I belong to Paul,' and another, 'I belong to Apollos,' **are you not merely Men?**"

You see, what Paul is actually saying is that his desire for the believer is to discover that '*I am more than an ordinary, mere Man!*'

God through His Word, the gospel, expounded upon in the New Testament Scriptures, desires to reveal to me the face of my new birth in the spirit realm, in Christ Jesus!

Even though we walk in the flesh, *even though I carry this meatbox with me in my time on this planet,* **there is much more to me than just a physical Man!**

We need to understand very clearly here that the Scriptures do not speak of two natures in one Man!

Religion often got confused when they looked at someone's behavior who was supposed to be a so called *"born again"* believer. They thought, *'Well, maybe it's just the old nature that is still manifesting.'* Listen; if that were true, then that would mean that **half of that person would go to heaven *while the other half goes to hell!***

This cannot be! Ha… ha… ha…

Jesus and James both make it plain that not even trees have two natures, amen!

What Paul is saying here is that **his desire for the believer is *to believe fully!***

His desire for the believer is to discover the reality of the face of his birth, of his spirit birth, of his new birth, there in Christ Jesus in that work of redemption! Not going away from that and going about and always forgetting again; forever forgetting what manner of Man they are! Not forever allowing something else's belief, someone else's opinion to shape and shake them; allowing someone else to so intimidate them, in their belief in the faith of

God, that they would have to revert back and suddenly just have to act like an ordinary Man again!

He says that his desire for the believer is *that they would continue to measure their life in terms of the new birth! That they would measure their life in terms of the fact that Christ indwells them!* **So that their mind can now be so renewed through the knowledge of who they are through that work of redemption;** *through the knowledge of who they are in Christ, so much so that their conduct would bear witness to that and bring testimony to that!*

Praise God!

Hallelujah!

We, the believers, *are the extension of the incarnation!*

Every year we ignorantly celebrate Christmas, but Christmas is really the celebration of the incarnation! Christmas and Christianity is the celebration of *the Word that* **became flesh!**

What was lost in the flesh, *God preserved in the Word!* What was lost in the flesh, *God preserved in that Logos,* **ready to be revealed in the last days!** **And I thank God that** *those last days* <u>*came*</u>*. The fullness of time* <u>**has come**</u>*; the Word was revealed! That Logos; the Word,* **became flesh** *and lived amongst us,* **and dwelt within us!**

46

I say again: **What was lost in the flesh, God preserved in the Word, in the Logos; in Christ!**

And so the Word again restored to the flesh what the flesh lost through the Fall!

So now in our faith today, we are no longer anticipating a prophetic word yet to become flesh! **No, we are celebrating the Word that was born amongst us, _and revealed to be within us_!**

And **we beheld Him!**

We beheld His glory!

And we beheld _our glory_ _there in Him!_

Clearly revealed _there in Him!_

On display in the Word _made flesh_!

And now God's desire for us is **to live _in the very testimony_ of that Word that became flesh!** He desires for us **to live our lives _in that testimony_!**

God's desire for you is to daily experience _the eternal,_ the super-natural, _as YOUR_ testimony!

If we are talking about measuring 2014 or our future **_in the light of His investment in us,_ then we cannot afford _to limit our view of ourselves_ to that of mere Men! We cannot** afford *to limit ourselves* to being mere Men! We cannot afford *to submit ourselves* to jealousies and strife and ordinary things. **It will distract us from God's purpose for our life!**

*If you accommodate jealousy in your life **it only means that you measure yourself with the wrong opinion!***

*If you accommodate disappointment or resentment or bitterness and unforgiveness or any form of sin and ugliness, **it means you are comparing yourself and measuring yourself by the wrong measure! You are measuring yourself with an incorrect inferior measure! It's the wrong measure!***

Chapter 4

The LIFE Made Manifest!

Please go with me now 1 John 1:1,

*"That which was **from the beginning** which we have heard, which we have seen with our eyes, which we have looked upon, and touched with our hands **concerning the Word of life**,"*

"The life was made manifest…"

I love this testimony of John. You know, he could give us a fairly accurate description of what Jesus looked like in the flesh, *because after all, he walked so closely with Him and so close to Him.*

He wrote this letter, by the way, 60 years later in history, after Jesus ascended to His Father and our Father. John was already around 90 years of age. But he didn't write from memory, trying to accurately remember history. No, describing Jesus from a fleshly point of view, from a historical reference, *from a flesh reference* was not his goal.

John desired to so communicate *his present day reality, his present tense experience,* with the rest of the believers, *and anyone else who would care to read his letter,* **so that they too would tap into, and be drawn into,** *the manifestation of the life* **of the Word,** *the very life of the Word, and not just a dry, boring old letter,* or a mere physical, historical description!

Verse 2 says,

"The life was made manifest, and we saw it and testify to it, and proclaim to you, the eternal life, which was with the Father and was made manifest to us!"

What I want to say about this scripture is that, if we anticipate in this year we live in, or the year to come, or in our future yet to come, even in the eternal future yet unknown, *if we anticipate, testimony upon testimony, tangible testimony,* we really need to consider in our hearts that *the tangible* **IS** *merely the revelation of, or the byproduct of, what we hear!* **It's the revelation of what I hear – the revealing of it,** *the byproduct of what I hear!* **That tangible experience in my spirit, as well as the tangible manifestation of it in the flesh** **IS** *the product of the Word!* *The Word precedes the tangible! The truth of the gospel revealed, grasped, and understood,* **precedes the tangible!**

Often I hear people complain that, *'Well, brother, there's a lack of testimony in my life, I don't seem to be able to live consistently in the experience of these things; it somehow doesn't*

50

work for me. I just don't see enough evidence of it, so it must not be true. Or, God must not want to answer my prayers and do it for me! Maybe I have a flawed design or something! Or, I know, maybe I'm too stupid to figure this stuff out! I just don't understand this lack of testimony in my life! Brother Rudi, I haven't experienced a miracle for weeks now, what is wrong? There must be something wrong!'

Do you know what I'm actually hearing when I hear that? I'm hearing only one thing. I'm hearing: **'I haven't had an encounter in the Word, a faith-encounter in the truth of the Word for weeks! I haven't had an encounter in the Scriptures; I haven't had an encounter with God in His Word for weeks!'**

Listen, you don't need to look for the tangible if the Word of truth is abiding in you. You don't need to look for the tangible if the Word Himself is abiding in your heart!

Why do I say that?

Because what you hear, what you are fully engaged in and meditating upon *will inspire in your spirit a faith. It will inspire in your spirit* **that faith of God that will become a vision within you, and you will see it, you will begin to grasp it, and believe it, and it will become more and more truth to you, more and more real; a living reality! It will** *become more and more tangible! You will experience it within your spirit! You will experience that intimate encounter; that sweet fellowship, that constant oneness with God in your spirit. And then the testimony of the eternal and of the super-natural will follow spontaneously!*

The tangible is a product *of the abiding Word! And the testimony of that eternal realm you abide in will follow, spontaneously and consistently!*

Hallelujah!

And let me tell you that **then** *no contradiction will ever again be able to limit your testimony!*

The Bible does not say,

"If you walk in the truth of the Word, there will never arise any difficulty against you!"

No. But it does say,

"In all these things we remain more than conquerors!"

"...In all these things!"

And the secret to our victory is our abiding in Him; it is *the place the Word holds in our hearts and our mouths; in our constant conversation!*

The secret to our victory is that faith of God, the Word, which our constant focus *imparts to us!*

This is the victory that overcomes the world: *FAITH.* **Even our faith; <u>the very faith of God</u>**!

The secret of our victory is **remembering** what **manner of Man we are!**

That's the secret: *Not forgetting what manner of Man we are!*

I have faced various times of affliction in my own life, and yes even after I became a Christian; *especially after I became a Christian.*

During this last time of affliction that came upon me, that scripture where Paul says, *"… this slight, momentary affliction"* became so precious to me, especially after I read that and immediately began to consider in my heart, *'Now what exactly was it that Paul compared that affliction with? I mean, what was it that caused him to be able to put it in perspective and call it "slight" and "momentary"?'*

You see, because usually we compare affliction with affliction and say, *'This one is worse than that one.'*

'You tell me of your old sad story and I'll tell you of mine!' Oh, *'You think you've had it bad, man, let me tell you, I've had it worse!'*

And there we go, and we compare our sad stories of 2013. The problem is that the more you compare it, *the more it intimidates you!*

But when Paul considers everything that has come against him, **he doesn't consider it for very long. In fact, he refuses to consider it at all.**

Let me tell you, **some terrible things came against Paul in his life!** *But he never considered it for very long* **before coming to a very clear and definite faith-conclusion!**

There were the times where he was adrift on the open sea, you know, not lying on a comfortable floating device with a cool glass of ice tea in his hand and a nice umbrella to protect him from the sun. No, *in the middle of severe storms, adrift, hanging in there for dear life!* And it wasn't a nice gold-inlaid piece of shipwreck he was hanging on to either!

Ha… ha… ha…

No, we don't even know if he had a piece of plank to hold on to! Most likely his eyes scanned the horizon from time to time and looking all around him, like so many of us would do, looking for those dreaded shark fins sticking up out of the water.

Ha… ha… ha…

But listen now, *he knew that his destiny in life was much larger than any temporal*

54

setback! **He knew and understood that he was born of another kind;** *that he was born from above!* *He knew* **he was more than just an ordinary man!**

Hallelujah!

There were times that he was attacked by robbers. They wanted his money and would just as soon kill him for it.

Listen that wasn't getting persecuted for his faith; he was simply attacked for his money.

So there are many things, *natural things,* not spiritual things, *just natural things* he faced and that came against him!

But he knew that any affliction, any natural affliction and disaster that the newspapers would call *"acts of God,"* and would go to town on and embellish and amplify and write large pages on, telling us the gory details, exactly how it happened, and when and where it happened, and who was involved in what happened, and what else happened in connection with it, or as a result of it. And the news media would drag it out as a news-worthy event and story, glorifying that horrific event for weeks and weeks, glorifying disaster, and glorifying the devil!

But you see, Paul knew that that affliction; that natural affliction, and even afflictions and attacks of a spiritual nature; **whatever affliction it might be,** he knew that,

"Whatever has come against me is but slight and momentary"

"It is small. It is momentary in the light of this eternal glory; in comparison with this eternal weight of glory I am enjoying in my spirit!"

Hallelujah!

So, if you want to measure your year, your past year, or your current year, even your future year, **you need to have a measure that is greater and larger than someone else's experience** of yesteryear, or even just last week!

Listen; don't get hung up on your past, or someone else's past! Interpret your past, interpret 2013 and then interpret 2014, even 2015 and beyond, *in the light of **His investment in you!***

*Interpret it **in the light of His prevailing LIFE in you, which comes from the word of life, the truth of the gospel, abiding and prevailing in you!***

Chapter 5

From The Beginning Was the Word!

But let's get back to 1 John now. So John says there in 1 John 1:2,

"That life that has been made manifest to us has become our testimony!"

The word says,

"...we hold fast to that confession of faith; that faith conversation!"

He says,

"...we embrace that testimony fully!"

He says that,

"...the tangible testimony begins with what we have heard from the beginning;"

"...what we have heard about that which was form the beginning!"

Listen, the beginning of your testimony is the Word! It is the revelation of that which was from the beginning! From the beginning was the Word! You make sure that word of Christ;

that word concerning your true identity and design, manifested, restored, and redeemed; make sure that that word concerning your redemption, the truth of it, *dwells in you richly! Make sure it dwells richly **in your heart!** Embrace it fully,* not just in your mind. **Embrace it fully *in your heart!* Embrace it with your spirit! Embrace it with your faith!**

Don't wait for a crisis before you get into the Scriptures, into the truth and the reality of these things; into the truth and reality of your redemption. ***Don't wait for a crisis before you get into these things <u>and make them yours</u>!*** No! Get into the Word daily! Abide in the Word! Abide in the Truth! Abide in God! **And Him in you!**

Then Paul says,

"Having done all to stand, stand therefore!"

He says,

"…STAND in the evil day!"

Stand so that when the evil day suddenly comes, **you're STANDING!** The day of attack finds you **STANDING! Standing STRONG in the fortitude, which the truth of the gospel affords you. Standing STRONG in Christ, in His love, and in His power to sustain you, leaning heavily upon Him, the strong One, in His enablement; in His strength, in His working *within you, supplying you with His STRENTH!***

58

That scripture we considered in James Chapter 1 *speaks of the Word that reveals the face of my birth.*

And when I hear that Word, I am not to deceive myself! **You see, it's possible to encounter the Word, to HEAR the Word, *and yet still not to experience its benefits.***

Just like Israel of old: They wandered around in circles in the desert for 40 years *until they all died.* They never did enter the Promised Land **because they did not mix the word they heard with faith!** I remind you that only two of them entered the Promised Land. And why? Because, while the rest were filled with fear and unbelief, those two chose rather **to consider the word of God, and to believe the word of God <u>as a greater reality</u>** *than what their natural eyes could tell them, or even than what their fears and doubts could try to tell them and intimidate them with!*

Just like those men that Paul spoke of in 1 Corinthians Chapter 3. **I mean, they were people that were birthed,** that got **brought into the things of God by the incorruptible seed of the Word, *and yet they continued to live like ordinary men!* They continued in their lives, in their lifestyle dominated by circumstances, dominated by temporal things, by lusts and passions, even by the empty dreams that natural Man occupies his heart and mind and time and life with!**

They were dominated by these things and they were restricted in their faith!

And so God's desire to communicate the fullness of Christ *through them,* the maturity of Jesus, the maturity of faith and love, the maturity of that Divine nature and that life, that abundant life, *life more abundantly; that desire of God to manifest and communicate that fullness, that maturity, through them, was frustrated!*

But listen, it's the Word becoming flesh in our hearts, coming alive in us, that becomes that tangible testimony!

And you know, it was so precious, *in the midst of my affliction,* to consider it, in the light of Paul's considering of it and his faith-conclusion he came to, and **to then experience the greater reality of the Word of truth, the gospel of my salvation for myself!**

It became so personally precious to consider the greater reality of it, and how it's greater than any disease, greater than what the doctors could say about my so called condition, greater even than what it felt like and looked like in the natural, greater than pain even, severe pain even.

Faith's vision prevails above the natural!

Faith's vision subdues the natural!

During one of my afflictions I went into the hospital and the Lord gave me an assurance, a very sure word in my heart that I was going to come out of that hospital with a blessing, *with more than just my healing!*

You know, often we may encounter a contradiction to our life, *and the only thing we're hoping for is survival.* I mean, everything in us just wants to get through this affliction or this trial and just feel normal again, just so that everything is just fine again!

But God quickened my spirit, and He said to me, *'Rudi, don't limit your miracle to just having your health restored to you!'*

There is a principle in this that I want you to get, *so read carefully and understand and hear clearly!*

Often we even encounter some financial setback perhaps, *and our faith is just to just get through this thing again.*

But **God** said to me, *'Rudi, **don't limit yourself to the natural!**'*

And He says the same thing to you now, as He said to me then:

'I want to give you the spoils of this battle!'

'I want to so turn the tables on the enemy that he would be totally bewildered and confused and utterly defeated - devastated

even that he ever even tried such a foolish act to bring this thing against your body!'

I went into that hospital and I said, *'Lord, the only spoils I'm interested in are the lives of others!'*

And God began to open the doors to that spoil. He gave me exactly what I wanted. He began to open the door to it through conversation with others there, speaking into the hearts of some of the staff there, some of those medical doctors and nurses, and the hearts of some of those patients.

And I can still remember what a precious time I had that last morning with the head of that hospital who took such good care of me there, and he asked me to send him CD's and DVD's and any material I have containing this beautiful, accurate gospel message! He said he wanted to share it with the world, starting with the closed-circuit television feed he has throughout that hospital in Malawi. And I just began to rejoice in the Lord with him, with big crocodile tears running down both of our faces, thanking God for divine appointments and knowing that our Daddy works together everything for our benefit!

God has opened a tremendous door there for me in the country of Malawi and now in that hospital also, for the Word! And I've come back with the spoils, with the opportunity to speak into other people's lives who are lying in that same place of affliction without the hope that we have; *without the faith substance that we have.* So often I find that when people are in crisis *their ears are open to hear!*

And now I want to encourage you right here in this book, as you anticipate the rest of 2014 or 2015 even, and as we as a local church body together, or even as the body of Christ together at large, consider and anticipate 2014 or 2015 or beyond, that we look at that future **in the light of the faith of God *that inspires us to live above the ordinary!***

Not just waiting for another month to come, but saying and *determining in our hearts,*

'God, today, I believe the tangible, miraculous, super-natural evidence of You, of Your reality and Your nearness, Your abiding presence in my life!'

Do you know where that encounter, that tangible experience begins?

In the beginning was the Word! It begins with that Word; with the truth of the gospel! What we have heard, not just with our natural ears, *but with our spiritual ears,* what we have seen, not just with our physical eyes, *but with our spiritual eyes, **the eyes of understanding, the eyes of faith,*** what we have **looked upon and focused upon;** *what we have beheld in the Word, what we have gazed upon concerning the truth of the gospel, concerning the Word of Life, concerning*

***the manifestation of that Life in Christ,
being given to us!*** **That is where that
encounter; that tangible experience begins!**

Listen; make that Word your vision!

See the heart of God in the gospel!

See the Word; see Jesus!

See it all made flesh!

See God Himself for who He is!

See the truth!

See yourself then also for who you are!

See yourself revealed in Him; in Christ Jesus!

See that truth!

Believe that truth; embrace that truth fully!

See its legality, and its reality!

Behold it!

Behold the Word of truth, the gospel of your
salvation which happened in Christ; in that
marvelous demonstration of His eternal love for
you in the act of redemption!

Ponder it!

Digest it!

Embrace it fully!

Believe it fully!

And you will have the most extra ordinary, *super-natural life you could ever dream to live!*

Ha… ha… ha… Hallelujah!

Just ask any man who truly lives and believes the Word! *There is daily super-natural feedback there! And testimony upon testimony!*

Chapter 6

God's Faith is the Substance of Things Hoped For!

I believe God wants to flood your life with testimony; with His testimony, with a strong witness that is alive within your spirit. He wants to flood your life with that testimony, **and with testimonies.**

And not next year, but this year, tomorrow even!

Ha... ha... ha...

But don't wait for the testimony to manifest before your mouth declares! It doesn't work that way, my friend!

The scriptures say in Hebrews 10,

"Let us hold fast to the confession of our hope..."

Now where in the world does hope fit in with faith? Hebrews 11, Verse 1 gives us the answer. It says,

"Now faith is the substance *...of things hoped for!"*

Hope speaks of the extension of your day and of your life; **the extension of it, the eternity of it, *the eternity of your LIFE in Him!* The LIFE that is larger than the now!**

Listen, we can never limit ZOE, the LIFE of God, *that LIFE that is in us.* **We can never limit that LIFE to time!** How can you even begin to measure eternity in terms of time? How can you measure ZOE in terms of time? How can you measure LIFE in terms of time? I **mean, consider the largeness, the enjoyment, the impact of the presence of God, in terms of time**… That measure becomes totally silly then!

I grew up in South Africa, and it is just absolutely beautiful in some areas of that country, especially down in the Cape and up the garden route, *and especially at the ocean there (in my opinion it is some of the most beautiful scenery anywhere on earth)!* And of course I have been to some places here in America and especially down in Florida at some of those turquoise waters and snow white beaches *that are almost just as beautiful.* But it is a different beauty, it has a beauty all its own! And at times, whether you are down there at the beaches in South Africa or here at the beaches and turquoise waters of Florida, at times you just want to capture in your mind and in your memory and in your heart, everything you see. I mean, it is so beautiful that you just want to stop and stare for a minute or two, and you just want to weep! You see, you are standing there, and you are trying to somehow consider the beauty of what God has given you in creation!

But you know, it never ceases to amaze me, the limits of the senses. You see, your senses can only approve of something in terms of a very restricted measure. I mean, how beautiful must the sun be in its setting to be the perfect sunset in your estimation? And what must you be able to fit into your day in order to make it the perfect day?

I almost always laugh at Carmen and myself when we go on holiday, because we always want to do so many things, all in one day! How much enjoyment and how many things must you be able to fit into and squeeze into a holiday to really make it, you know, *the perfect holiday* to where you can say that *it was really worth it! It was really worth the time and money and energy spent!*

What is your measure of enjoyment, your measure of appreciation?

I enjoy the ability we have in our senses to capture beauty and hold it for a while. But one day as I was still standing on the beach and doing that exact thing, *suddenly God spoke to my heart and He said to me that **His presence far exceeds any experience that we could ever capture here in the physical realm!***

God's presence in you, in your heart, *exceeds any experience you can ever know that has* beauty in it, **that has weight in it, that has quality and worth to it; that has some kind of value in it!**

The ZOE that we enjoy (ZOE is the Greek word *for the LIFE that God births within us through His truth, through the gospel, through the Word that was from the beginning, through the Word of our salvation*) That ZOE is an enjoyment of a specific unmeasurable quality of life. It's a life that cannot be bought; *it's priceless! It's a life that is larger than time!* **It's a life that is larger than what you can calculate in the senses, or in terms of minutes and hours!**

So many people live their whole lives within the boundaries of their job-description, **within the boundaries of their occupation or their career, 'I'm worth so much an hour!' And they limit their whole life to what they're worth in Man's evaluation of talent and abilities!**

Listen, discover the wealth of your life in God's sight, *and begin to live the limits, the full measure of His estimation of you!* **Discover that boundary-less limit!**

God wants to hear you say,

'God, this day is the day that the Lord has made! I refuse to limit my joy today to just one good meal I'm going to have tonight when I get home, or when it's finally Friday, and we get to go out to eat!'
70

'God I refuse to limit my joy to that next car I'd like to buy!'

'...to that new job or that nice retirement I'm hoping to get.'

'...but Father, I want to live daily in the fullness of joy that is to be found in your presence!'

'...at Your right hand there is fullness of joy, and there are pleasures forevermore!'

'Father I would much rather measure my life with Your measure.'

'Father I want to measure my life in terms of my inheritance;'

'...in terms of the inheritance You have given me,'

'...for surely the measuring lines have fallen for me in very pleasant places, and in my enjoyment of that, goodness and mercy shall follow me all the days of my life! I will dwell secure in the heart of my Father forever and ever!'

'...surely my life is hidden secure with Christ in God!'

'...surely my life is in Christ Jesus alone!'

'...surely Christ is my life!'

'...surely my life is preserved and sealed in Him! Time and disaster cannot diminish what I have and enjoy in God!'

Listen, Paul sat there in that ugly old prison **and he was not robbed of his joy, because he knew that no temporal circumstance could limit his approach before the Father and his enjoyment and his access into the very presence of God and into the fullness of His presence!** He knew that no temporal circumstance could rob him **of that enjoyment and limit his abiding place in Him!**

So in this book I want to leave you with the challenge that 2014 and 2015 and our whole future ahead of us is ours *in terms of what faith can see and partake of!*

Hebrews 11:1,

"Now faith is <u>the substance</u> of things hoped for!"

In Romans 5:5 Paul says,

"Now that kind of hope, that faith, will not disappoint you, because God's love has been quickened in your heart, brought to life by the Holy Spirit!"

So often the people who hope for many things are often more disappointed than not.

But listen God says,

*"**This** hope, this faith, will not disappoint you!"*

Why not?

"…because the love of God has been awakened in your heart!"

This has become such a reality to us in our church fellowship lately!

You know, we can get so technical in our faith definitions sometimes. How you've got to put out your faith for this and put out your faith for that, and believe God for your healing, and believe for this and that, and it's all wonderful and good, our trying to doctrinally define things. But actually, it is much simpler than that. We can so easily make things so complicated sometimes, needlessly!

The revelation of the Bible, the revelation of this Word, the revelation of the gospel *is the revelation of God's favor!*

It's the revelation of God's favor towards you!

And if you discover through that truth of the gospel God's favor upon you, if you discover through God's faith, His favor upon you, His intense love for you, *you at the same time discover access into everything that God has purposed for you!*

Chapter 7

The Evidence of His LIFE in You!

Let me just read to you Romans 5:1,

"Therefore since we are justified by faith…"

You see, we are not justified by our own merit!

We are justified by faith; by God's faith.

Why do I say that?

Because God believes in the merit of His Son Jesus on our behalf!

So this should read this way really,

"Therefore, since we are justified by God's faith,"

Not our own faith, but God's faith, amen.

"…we have peace with God;"

"Since therefore we are justified by God's faith,"

"…that's why we have peace with God!"

That means, no problems between us; *no negative vibes,*

"...through our Lord Jesus Christ."

Verse 2 says,

"Through Him we have obtained access into this grace in which we stand!"

"And we rejoice in our (living) *hope* (it's become a reality in Him, amen!);"

"...we rejoice in that hope of sharing in the glory of God (right now by our faith, amen!)."

Our faith is awakened by His truth. Our faith is the fruit of seeing His faith; of grasping and understanding what God believes about us, and what God believed happened in the work of redemption. Comprehending and embracing fully what God already did for us, and declares about us, in Jesus. Our faith is merely a positive response; *an embrace of that faith; the very faith of God.*

Verse 3,

"More than that, (because of that, or added to that, or on top of that) *we rejoice in* (the middle of) *sufferings* (we rejoice **in spite of sufferings**) *knowing that the suffering produces..."*

It produces what?

"...it produces endurance;"

In other words: **It produces a response out
of us** *from out of the faith imparted to us
through the truth of the Word.* That
response that is produced from inside of us is
called *endurance!*

"And that endurance..."

Verse 4,

"That endurance (that faith, that total
persuasion, that steadfastness, that constant
reality we live in) *produces* **evidence!"**

My RSV Bible says *"character"* there, but the
Greek word is clearly the word used for
"evidence".

And remember, we have just been talking
about *tangible testimony!* God wants every
one of us, *yes; you included,* to daily
experience tangible testimony, **the tangible
witness of the Spirit in our hearts; a living
faith, a constant encounter within us, a
daily tangible testimony in our lives! He
wants every one of us to show evidence of
the grace of God,** *evidence of God's
miraculous working, first and foremost in
our hearts, but also then in our lives!*

And it's not just going to come your way, you
know, maybe one day, maybe never, you

know, who knows. **But no, it will come underline immediately as a result of your embrace of the truth of the gospel in your heart; as a result of the indwelling Word!**

So *this endurance produces evidence* **or faith-encounter!**

I think the Greek word there is the word, DOKIMOS where we get our English word *"document"* from. That word speaks of *that which passes the necessary test or scrutiny,* thus the words **approved, accepted, tried and true** immediately comes to mind. It thus speaks of **the proof**, or **a tangible legal reality**, or **the legal result**, such as *a receipt, or a document of ownership,* something *concrete and tangible and real.*

"...and that evidence (or that faith has substance to it, and so it) *produces more hope."*

And now Paul says in Verse 5,

"...that hope does not disappoint us..."

Why?

"...it does not disappoint us, because the love of God has been imparted to our hearts!"

Listen, it's the abundance of God's love towards you, *revealed deep in your inner man, embraced there in your heart;* it's that knowledge *of the abundance of God's love towards you,* that knowing and believing *the love God has for you,* which will sustain you in suffering! It will sustain you in everything that comes against you!

You see, if the enemy can bring something against you, and together with that thing, *bring a little bit of condemnation, or bring a little bit of suspicion towards God,* just a little bit of accusation against you or against God into your mind and into your heart, or even against someone else for being the cause of it or instrumental in it ...if that thing coming against you, that thing, that enemy, can bring with it and introduce that accusation and that condemnation, *just a little bit of it even,* **then that thing will develop a hold on your spirit and defeat you!**

Listen Paul says (actually the Word of God through Paul says),

"Nothing can separate us from His love!"

If the love of God is imparted and grasped in the rich abundance of God's measure in your heart, *and you walk in the consciousness of that love for you, in the consciousness of God's love for you* **and His favor upon you,** *then hope will not disappoint you!*

Your vision for 2014 and 2015 and beyond **will be more than just a dream;** *it will be the enjoyment of a tangible reality!* **And that**

vision will then also become tangible reality even in this natural dimension we live in!

And do you know what will happen through the fruit of your testimony, through the fruit of that reality you live in? *Others will taste and see that the Lord is good!*

Listen, we need to touch this world with our testimony, *and through our testimony!* We need to touch this world with the evidence, *the fruit,* of our lives, **with our enjoyment in that faith of God! We need to touch them with *the fruit* of that faith!**

They are not all farmers; many of them aren't. I mean, they won't go buy bags of seed, *so don't just show up and throw out scriptures at them!* Give them the fruit! The sweetness that you enjoy! **Listen, God has concealed the seed *in the fruit!* They'll taste that fruit and the fruit <u>will attract them</u> to encounter the same seed, the same resource, the same secret, the secret of your <u>life</u>!**

The secret of your life is your union with Christ in God, *enjoying that union, enjoying intimacy, enjoying that love,* **there in the secret place of thunder, in your bosom, *as you are abiding in your Father's bosom!***

If we make this our focus, abiding in the bosom of our Father, of our Daddy, focusing on our acceptance in the Beloved, on the immense extravagant love of God for us, if we make that our enjoyment, *I believe our testimony will ignite many right now, this year already!*

Not four more months and then comes the harvest. No! Lift up your eyes, the fields is white unto harvest!

Revival is not still coming; *it is here!*

I believe for the largest harvest we've ever considered possible, *not next year, **this year!*** Not next week, **today already!** Not a long way off, **now already!**

If we make this our focus: Our enjoyment of the Word, our enjoyment of the truth of the gospel, *I really believe our testimony **will ignite many!** And we can then **reap** the biggest harvest **this year,** in terms of men and women!* **We don't have to wait for next year!** *I believe it with all my heart!*

Sometimes, even in the Charismatic circles, even in the revival circles, even in the grace circles, ***we are still waiting for God to do it; for God to do something, something spectacular!***

*'**Oh, God, 2014 or 2015 maybe, Lord, 2014 is Your year, You do it this year Lord, please!**'*

God did it over 2,014 years ago, **it's now our turn,** *it's now your turn, amen.* **He wants your faith, the testimony of your faith,** *to draw them in!*

Hallelujah!

Thank you Father, thank you Jesus, thank you Holy Spirit *that You work through us in this hour!* Thank you for that responsibility You have given us; *thank you for that honor!*

It is such a privilege to have God be at work in us and through us both to will and to do of His good pleasure!

Have you found how quickly people are open to listen to a testimony, *or to someone sharing what they truly enjoyed,* rather than to a scriptural principle that I studied this morning?

Listen, that's God's strategy for His Church.

It's the testimony of His grace! That testimony <u>manifested;</u> revealed to you, revealed in your life ...that testimony becomes <u>manifest;</u> because of what you hear in the closet; *in your inner ear!*

Take Isaiah 50:4 as a daily scripture in your life this year, from now on forever, amen!

Hallelujah!

It says,

"Morning by morning He awakens my ear to hear as those who are taught,"

"...and therefore He has given me the tongue of the learned,"

82

"...that I may know how to sustain him who is weary with a word; with the Word **(with the truth of the Gospel, with the love of God for every single individual on the face of this earth, and especially directed towards the weary ones)***!"*

Listen; His Word will not fail you!

Hallelujah!

The Bible says,

"Heaven and earth will pass away..."

What a disappointment that will be, *especially to those who have their all invested in this earth.*

Ha... ha... ha...

But God says His Word will not pass away! His Word concerning me will not pass away! This Word of my redemption, **this Word of my design and true identity restored, this Word of my sonship restored to me,** *this word of no separation, this word of my complete union and seamless oneness with Him,* <u>**this**</u> <u>**Word**</u> **will not pass away! And it will not return unto Him void either!**

I'm not an ordinary Man!

Say it with me,

State it: **I am not an ordinary Man!**

Say it!

I AM NOT AN ORDINARY PERSON!

I REFUSE TO LIVE AN ORDINARY LIFE!

I DETERMINE TODAY TO LIVE MY LIFE IN THE LIGHT OF GOD'S INVESTMENT IN ME!

Hallelujah!

We worship You Lord!

We thank you Father!

We praise You Jesus!

Father, we thank you that we know today *that it is Your faith **that finds expression through us*** as we live a life of FAITH!

*…**as we walk by FAITH and not by sight!***

We thank you Father, thank you for The Greater One who indwells us!

Father, as we anticipate our day, today, and tomorrow, and this year, and the next one Father, **there is a rising excitement within us!**

Thank you for that Father! Amen.

I want to encourage any one of you who may have read this book, and yet you have never made a personal commitment in your heart to this Jesus *who loves you so much that He was willing to die to prove it,* hey, don't put this book down and walk away thinking about it.

No, think about it now, **and just yield to His extravagant love for you, and make that commitment right now.**

And if you'd like someone to stand in prayer agreement with you, *feel free to contact us on Facebook or via our website.*

I am sure someone on the other end would just love to minister to you and send you on your way blessed and fulfilled in Christ.

Even if you have any other need whatsoever, they can also pray and come in agreement with you about that!

In closing, I urge you to get yourself a copy of the *Mirror Study Bible.* It is the best translation of the Scriptures from the original Greek that I have ever read, because it reveals the nuances and intimate details of God's heart and Paul's gospel the clearest. It's available online at Barnes & Nobel and several other book sellers.

If you want me or someone a part of our team to come to where you are, *anywhere in the world,* and give a talk, or teach you and some of your friends *about the gospel message and these redemption realities,* simply contact us at www.LivingWordIntl.com, or you can always find me on Facebook.

If your life has changed as a result of reading this book, *please write to me and let me know.*

I would love to share your joy, *so that my joy in writing this book may be full!*

That which was from the
beginning,

which we have heard
(**with our spiritual ears**),
which we have seen
(**with our spiritual eyes**),
which we have looked upon
(**beheld, focused our attention
upon**),
and which our hands have also
handled
(**which we have also
experienced**),

concerning the Word of life,

we declare to you,

that you also may have this
fellowship with us;

and truly our fellowship is with
the Father
and with His Son Jesus Christ.

And these things we write to you
that your joy may be full.
~ 1John 1:1-4

About the Author

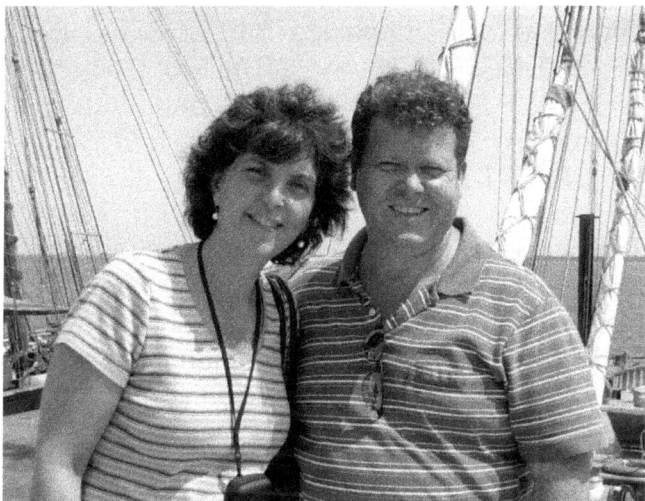

Rudi & Carmen Louw together oversee: Living Word International.

They also travel and minister both locally and internationally.

Rudi was born and raised in the country of South Africa, while Carmen grew up in Cortland, New York.

They function in the ministry of reconciliation (2 Corinthians 5:18-21) and flow strongly with the Holy Spirit and His anointing to teach, preach, prophesy, heal, and whatever is needed to touch people's lives with the reality of God's love and power.

God has given them keen insight into what He has to say to mankind in the work of redemption concerning the revelation and restoration of humanity's true identity.

Therefore they emphasize THE GOSPEL, IN CHRIST REALITIES, the GRACE of God, the WORD OF RIGHTEOUSNESS, *and all such eternal truths essential to salvation and living the CHRIST-LIFE.*

They have been granted this wisdom and revelation into the knowledge of God by the Spirit of Truth; that resurrected Spirit of Jesus Christ, *to establish and strengthen believers in the faith of God, and to activate them in ministering to others.*

Not only are people set free from the poison and bondage of sin, condemnation and all kinds of intimidation, (upheld, strengthened and reinforced by age old religious ideas born out of ignorance) **but many are brought into a closer more intimate relationship with Father God, as Daddy**, through accurate teaching and unveiling of the gospel message, prophetic words, healings and miracles.

Rudi & Carmen are closely knitted together with many other effective Christians, church fellowships, and groups of believers who share the same revelation and passion *to impart the truth of the gospel to others, and so **to impact and transform the world we live in with the LOVE and POWER of God**.*

www.ingramcontent.com/pod-product-compliance
Lightning Source LLC
Chambersburg PA
CBHW060406050426
42449CB00009B/1921